THE BIBLE CURE®

FOR

WEIGHT LOSS AND MUSCLE GAIN

DON COLBERT, M.D.

SILOAM PRESS

Living in Health—Body, Mind and Spirit

THE BIBLE CURE FOR WEIGHT LOSS AND MUSCLE GAIN
by Don Colbert, M.D.
Published by Siloam Press
A part of Strang Communications Company
600 Rinehart Road
Lake Mary, Florida 32746
www.siloampress.com

Library of Congress Catalog Card Number:
99-85844

International Standard Book Number:
0-88419-684-4

01 02 03 04   8 7 6 5
Printed in the United States of America

You Are
God's Masterpiece!

Before the finger of God touched the oceans with unimaginable creative power, God envisioned you in His heart. He saw you and all you could be one day through the power of His supernatural grace.

You are God's masterpiece, designed according to an eternal plan so awesome that it's beyond your ability to comprehend. Have you ever wondered what He saw in His mind when He created you? What was the perfection of purpose and plan He intended?

Now close your eyes and see yourself. For one moment you have no bondages, no imperfections, no shortcomings. Your body is as lean and healthy as it could possibly be. What do you look like? Is that the person God had in mind?

If you've struggled with obesity all of your life, you may not even be able to imagine yourself free of the bondage of unwanted fat. But God can. Don't you think that if God is powerful enough to create you and the entire universe that you see around you, that He is also able to help you overcome all of your personal bondages? Of course He is!

That's what this Bible Cure booklet is all about. It is a plan of godly principles, wisdom and scriptural advice to help deliver you from an unhealthy lifestyle and future ill health and to give you the freedom and joy of a healthy, fit, more attractive you!

You Are Not Alone

If you have a weight problem, you're not alone. Obesity, defined as being more than 20 percent above the ideal weight for height,[1] has reached almost epidemic proportions in the U.S., where approximately one in every three adults is now considered obese.

Children are not exempt. The epidemic of obesity impacts the lives of about one out of every five of our children.[2]

A Deadly Killer

Research tells us that in the United States, an estimated 300,000 deaths per year are attributed to obesity. Excess weight is threatening your life![3]

When compared to our total yearly health care bill of approximately $884 billion (in 1993 dollars), the 1990 direct and indirect costs associated with the burden, death, disability, products and services associated with obesity totaled approximately $100 billion. More than 45 percent of women and 25 percent of men are actively participating in some kind of weight-loss program.[4] These statistics simply mean that your excess weight can cost you both your health and your finances in the years to come.

Power for Success

This simple Bible Cure provides all you need for health and successful weight loss to help you become the person you saw when you closed your eyes. With fresh understanding, nutrition, exercise, vitamins and supplements, you can find all the physical elements you need for radical change. Mixed together with the power of God found in prayer and Scripture, you will discover strength for success that is beyond your own ability.

In this Bible Cure booklet you will

uncover God's divine plan of health
for body, soul and spirit
through modern medicine, good nutrition
and the medicinal power
of Scripture and prayer.

You will discover practical steps to take in each chapter:

As you learn about obesity, understand its causes and take the practical, positive steps detailed in this booklet, you will defeat obesity in your life and discover the abundant life promised by Jesus when He said, "My purpose is to give life in all its fullness" (John 10:10).

—DON COLBERT, M.D.

A BIBLE CURE PRAYER
FOR YOU

I pray that God will fill you with hope, encouragement and wisdom as you read this book. May He give you the will power to make healthy choices about your nutrition, exercise, attitudes and lifestyle. May He strengthen your resolve to maintain a healthy weight and not to overtax your body with excessive weight. I pray that you live a long and prosperous life walking in divine health so that you may serve and worship the Lord. Amen.

Chapter 1

Did You Know?— Understanding Obesity

The Bible instructs us to be wise in our eating habits: "Whatever you eat or drink or whatever you do, you must do all for the glory of God" (1 Cor. 10:31). The way you eat, drink and care for the body that God gave you can bring glory to Him for this wonderful gift.

Chances are that if you are struggling with obesity, you may have been waging a war with it all of your life. By now you realize that you need more than a good dieting program. You need power to enforce it. You need the strength it takes to change a lifetime of poor eating habits and the discipline to stay with it. This Bible Cure pathway to wholeness does not only provide the information necessary for a healthier, trimmer body, it also provides insight into an endless source of power to insure success. Stop limiting yourself to your own strength. The Bible reveals a better way:

> I can do everything with the help of Christ
> who gives me the strength I need.
> —Philippians 4:13

Gaining new power in your battle against obesity must begin with gaining fresh understanding of the causes for obesity.

Why We Eat Too Much

Being overweight has many causes. Some are biological. You might be predisposed to obesity through genetics and body metabolism. Some of the causes are psychological.

Emotional eating

You also may be emotionally dependent on food for comfort during times of stress, crisis, happiness, loneliness and a host of other emotions.

If overeating has an emotional component in your life, you probably grew up hearing statements like the following:

- "Eat something; it will make you feel better."

- "Clean your plate, or you can't leave the table."
- "If you're good, you will get dessert."
- "If you don't eat everything, you will be impolite to the host or hostess."
- "If you stop crying, I'll give you ice cream."

The list of unhealthy childhood motivations can be endless. But whether the causes of your weight problem are genetic or psychological, you are not bound to your past. Today is a new day, filled with fresh hope for an entirely new way of thinking and living. Begin considering what lifestyle factors might be contributing to your situation.

> *The unfailing love of the LORD never ends! By his mercies we have been kept from complete destruction. Great is his faithfulness; his mercies begin afresh each day.*
> —LAMENTATIONS 3:22–23

A sedentary lifestyle

Another cause of obesity is the increasingly sedentary lifestyle in our society. In an agricultural or industrial culture, hard work gives people plenty of exercise during the day. In our corporate, technological culture, we sit more at desks and in meetings. What about you?

Too much refined sugar and starch

Even though most Americans have decreased their fat intake dramatically, there is still a rise in obesity. According to the National Institute of Health, even though the dietary intake of fats and cholesterol is decreasing, the average weight of American young adults has increased by ten pounds. Before 1980 only one-fourth of the population was obese. However, today one-third of the population is obese. Even though most Americans have decreased their fat and many are switching to diet drinks, Americans continue to gain weight.

I believe one of the most important reasons for our epidemic of obesity is our high intake of both refined sugars and starches. The average consumption of refined sugar per year is one hundred fifty pounds per person.[1]

Take a look at how most of our bread is made. First the outer shell of the grain of wheat is removed. This is the bran or the fiber portion of the grain. The germ of the wheat is then removed; the germ contains the essential fats and vitamin E. These are removed to affect the shelf life of the bread. What is left over is the endosperm, which is the starch of the grain. This is then ground into a very fine powder. The powder of the grain, however, is not white, so then it is bleached with a bleaching agent.

With both the bran and the wheat germ no longer present, and after the bleaching process, very few vitamins remain. Therefore, man-made vitamins are then added back, along with sugar, salt, partially hydrogenated fats and preservatives. White bread is very constipating because it contains no fiber. Also, since it is highly processed when it is consumed, it is rapidly broken down into sugars, and this then causes high amounts of insulin to be secreted, putting a strain on the pancreas.

I believe that increased consumption of white bread, sugar, processed cereals and pasta is largely responsible for our epidemic of diabetes, high cholesterol, heart disease and obesity. In centuries past, these refined breads and sugars were given mainly to extremely rich and royal families. This is why many of the wealthy in those days were obese and suffered from diabetes and gout.

Sugar and Your Body

Contrary to popular opinion, eating fat does not necessarily make you fat. It's actually the way that your body stores fat that makes you gain weight. Overconsumption of carbohydrates and sugars stimulates your body's production of insulin— which is the body's fat storage hormone. Insulin lowers blood sugar levels when they are too high. However, it also causes the body to store fat.

For example, when you eat foods that are high in carbohydrates, such as breads, pasta, potatoes, corn and rice, the carbohydrate is changed into blood sugar, and in the presence of insulin it is then converted into blood fat by the liver. The fat in the blood is then stored away in fat cells.

Easier On Than Off

If you consume a lot of starch and sugar on a frequent basis, your insulin levels will remain high. If insulin levels remain high, your fat is then locked into your fat cells. This makes it very easy to gain weight and extremely difficult to lose weight. Elevated insulin levels prevent the body from burning stored body fat for energy. Most obese patients cannot break out of this vicious cycle because they are constantly craving starchy, sugary foods throughout the day, which keeps the insulin levels elevated and prevents the body from burning these stored fats.

The average person can store about 300–400 grams of carbohydrates in the muscles and about 90 grams in the liver. The stored carbohydrates are actually a stored form of glucose called glycogen. However, once the body storehouses are filled in the liver and muscles, any excess carbohydrates are then converted into fat and stored in fatty tissues.

Answer my prayers, O LORD, for your unfailing love is wonderful. Turn and take care of me, for your mercy is so plentiful. Don't hide from your servant; answer me quickly, for I am in deep trouble!
— PSALM 69:16–17

Exercise may not help you if you don't eat right. If you eat carbohydrates throughout the day, since the glycogen levels in your body are filled, all the excess carbohydrates will be converted to fat. The high insulin levels also tell the body not to release any of its stored fat. Therefore, you can work out for hours at a gym and still not lose fat because you are eating high amounts of carbohydrates and sugar throughout the day. Your body will store any excess carbohydrates as fat and not release any fat that is already stored.

Low blood sugar. To make matters even worse, when you consume sugar or starches frequently, especially cake, candy, cookies, fruit juices, ice cream or processed white flour, you may develop low blood sugar within a few hours after eating. Symptoms of this include spaciness, shakiness, irritability, extreme fatigue, headache, sweatiness, racing heart, extreme hunger or an extreme craving for something sweet or starchy.

Caught in a Trap

This creates a vicious cycle. If you don't eat something sweet or starchy every few hours, you will develop the symptoms of low blood sugar. This is a very important point. You can turn this entire situation around very easily by taking a very simple step.

Decrease the number of times each day you consume sugar and starches. By decreasing the number of times each day that you consume sweets, starches, snack foods, junk foods or high-carbohydrate foods, you can lower your insulin levels and turn off the main trigger that is telling the body to store fat and preventing the body from releasing fat.

When the brain doesn't get enough glucose,

you will get cravings. The brain requires a constant supply of glucose. When too much insulin is secreted, such as when you eat a snack that is high in sugar like a doughnut, a Coke or cookies, the pancreas then responds by secreting enough insulin to lower the sugar. Often too much insulin is secreted and lowers the sugar to a much lower level than acceptable, thus creating low blood sugar. Since the brain is not getting the glucose it requires, it sends out warning signals that include carbohydrate cravings, extreme hunger, mood swings, fatigue and problems concentrating. These signals cause the individual to reach for a sugar or starch "fix" in order to raise the blood sugar to a normal level, which will then be able to supply the brain with adequate glucose.

The Power of Glucagon

Glucagon is another hormone that works totally opposite than insulin works. Insulin is a fat-storing hormone, whereas glucagon is a fat-releasing hormone. In other words, glucagon will actually enable the body to release stored body fat from the fatty tissues and will permit your muscle tissues to burn your fat as the preferred fuel source instead of blood sugar.

How do you release this powerful substance into your body? It's easy. The release of glucagon is stimulated by eating a correct amount of protein in a meal along

My health may fail, and my spirit may grow weak, but God remains the strength of my heart; he is mine forever.
—PSALM 73:26

with the proper balance of fats and carbohydrates. We will look at this in greater detail later on.

When the level of insulin is high in the body, the level of glucagon is low. When glucagon is high, then insulin is low. When you eat a lot of sugar and starch, you raise your insulin levels and lower your glucagon, thus preventing fat from being released to be used as fuel. Too much sugar in the blood causes the brain to recognize the high sugar levels as fuel and shut down the body's mechanism for using your fat as fuel. By simply stabilizing your blood sugar, you can keep your glucagon levels elevated, which enables your body to burn off the extra fat. Thus, you'll begin to realize a more energetic, slimmer you!

Should You Count Calories?

Many people still say, "Why not count calories? A

calorie is a calorie." Most people believe that since fat has nine calories per gram and carbohydrates have only four calories per gram, then eating a gram of fat is much more fattening than eating a gram of carbohydrate. But the hormonal effects of fat are not nearly as dramatic as the hormonal effects of carbohydrates and sugars.

Fat will not stimulate insulin. However, sugars and starches will trigger dramatic releases of insulin, which is the most powerful fat-storing hormone. So don't count calories. Instead, be aware of how your body works. Keep in mind the powerful hormonal effects that sugars and starches have on both insulin, the fat-storing hormone, and on glucagon, the fat-releasing hormone.

The Bible says, "It is useless to spread the net in the eyes of any bird" (Prov. 1:17, NAS). That means you cannot capture a prey if it understands what's happening. By understanding this powerful truth about how your body actually works, you can avoid the trap of high blood sugar, being overweight and even diabetes. Now that you know, the power is in your hands!

Your Glycemic Index

How fast carbohydrates are absorbed into the

bloodstream is called the glycemic index. The glycemic index was originally developed for diabetics. It actually rates how quickly foods will raise the blood sugar levels. All foods are compared with pure glucose, which has a glycemic index of one hundred. If the glycemic index number is higher, that means that the blood sugar will be raised faster. If the glycemic index number is lower, the blood sugar will rise more slowly.

The higher the glycemic index number, the worse off you are. Lower numbers are good because they indicate

> *I love you,*
> *LORD; you are*
> *my strength.*
> —PSALM 18:1

that your body will have more time to handle the sugar in your bloodstream. This chart may help.

✓ A BIBLE CURE HEALTHFACT

Glycemic Index of Foods

EXTREMELY HIGH
(GREATER THAN 100)

GRAIN-BASED FOODS

Puffed rice
Millet
French bread

Corn flakes
Instant rice

VEGETABLES

Cooked parsnips
Instant potatoes
Borad beans (Fava Beans)

Baked russet potato
Cooked carrots

SIMPLE SUGARS

Maltose
Honey

GLYCEMIC STANDARD=100

White bread

HIGH (80–100)

GRAIN-BASED FOODS

Wheat bread
Whole-meal bread
Shredded wheat
Rye bread, crispbread
Brown rice
Sweet corn

Grape Nuts
Corn tortilla
Muesli
Rye bread, whole
Porridge oats
White rice

VEGETABLES

Mashed potatoes

Broiled new potato

FRUITS

Apricots
Banana
Mango

Raisins
Papaya

SNACKS

Corn chips
Crackers
Pastry

Mars bar
Cookies
Low-fat ice cream

MODERATELY HIGH (60–80)

GRAIN-BASED FOODS

Buckwheat	All Bran
Pumpernickel bread	Bulgur
White macaroni	White spaghetti
Brown spaghetti	

VEGETABLES

Yam	Sweet potato
Green peas, marrowfat	Frozen green peas
Canned baked beans	Canned kidney beans

FRUITS

Fruit cocktail	Grapefruit juice
Orange juice	Pineapple juice
Canned pears	Grapes

SNACKS

Oatmeal cookies	Potato chips
Sponge cake	

MODERATE (40–60)

VEGETABLES

Haricot (white) beans	Tomato soup
Brown beans	Lima beans
Dried green peas	Chickpeas (garbanzo)
Butter beans	Black-eyed peas
Kidney beans	Black beans

FRUITS

Orange	Apple juice
Pears	Apple

DAIRY

Yogurt	High-fat ice cream
Whole milk	2 percent milk
Skim milk	

LOW (LESS THAN 40)

GRAIN-BASED FOOD

Barley

Vegetables

Red lentils	Canned soybeans

FRUITS

Peaches	Plums

SIMPLE SUGARS

Fructose

SNACKS

Peanuts

The amount of fiber in your food, the amount of fat, how much sugar is in the carbohydrates and proteins all determine the glycemic index score of what you eat.

Three Types of Sugar

Three main types of simple sugars (called monosaccharides) make up all carbohydrates. These include:

- Glucose
- Fructose
- Galactose

Glucose is found in breads, cereals, starches, pasta and grains. Fructose is found in fruits, and galactose is found in dairy products. Plain sugar, or sucrose, is a disaccharide and consists of glucose and fructose joined.

The liver rapidly absorbs these simple sugars. However, only glucose can be released directly back into the blood stream. Fructose and galactose must first be converted to glucose in the liver to gain entrance into the blood stream. Thus, they are released at a much slower rate. Fructose, found primarily in fruits, has a low glycemic index compared to glucose and galactose.

Other Glycemic Foods

Fiber is a form of carbohydrate that is not absorbed. However, it does slow down the rate of absorption of other carbohydrates. Thus the higher the fiber content of the carbohydrate or starch, the more slowly it will be absorbed and enter the blood stream. White bread, which has no fiber, is absorbed rapidly. In fact, it has the same glycemic index as glucose.

When the carbohydrate you eat enters the blood-stream rapidly, your pancreas secretes a large amount of insulin. This insulin lowers the sugar level, but it also triggers the body to store fat.

I am overcome with joy because of your unfailing love, for you have seen my troubles, and you care about the anguish of my soul.
—PSALM 31:7

Most fruits have a low glycemic index except bananas, raisins, dates and other dried fruits. Almost all vegetables are low-glycemic foods except for potatoes, carrots, corn and beets.

Many high-glycemic foods are common snack foods. Almost all cereals, grains, pastas, breads, potatoes, corn, popcorn, chips, pretzels, crackers, bagels and other starches are high-glycemic carbohydrates. Therefore, you can easily see why people become obese, since these foods continue to trigger insulin release, and insulin continues to tell the body to store fat and keep it stored.

A Popcorn Problem

One patient arrived at my office weighing three hundred pounds. He claimed to have been on a low-fat diet for years, but continued to gain weight. When I questioned him about his dietary history, I learned that he ate a large bowl of popcorn each night before bed. This man just loved popcorn. He had once even joined "Popcorn Anonymous." Each evening both he and his mother would sit in front of the TV happily munching on popcorn for hours while his blood sugar level silently rose higher and higher.

The popcorn's high glycemic index caused surges of insulin to be released in his body. And the insulin told his body to store fat and keep it stored. He felt that he just couldn't lose weight, and he was right. His sugar levels were causing his fat to be locked into his body like a steel vault. Without knowing it, this man was signaling his body to store fat for hours every night.

> *You send rain on the mountains from your heavenly home, and you fill the earth with the fruit of your labor. You cause grass to grow for the cattle. You cause plants to grow for people to use. You allow them to produce food from the earth—wine to make them glad, olive oil as lotion for their skin, and bread to give them strength.*
> —PSALM 104:13–15

Little Mints With a Large Effect

Another woman came to my office who weighed two hundred thirty pounds. When I questioned her regarding her dietary history, her diet actually seemed very healthy. She was not eating a lot of fat, starches or sugars. She was not drinking soft drinks or any other sugary beverages. She was eating plenty of fruits and vegetables.

However, after questioning her further, I found out that she sucked on breath mints all day long. The sugary mints were enough to keep her blood sugar levels elevated and signal her body to store fat. Even though she was on a low-starch, low-fat diet that had plenty of fruits and vegetables, she continued to gain weight. When she eliminated her sugary breath mints and started on a walking program, she was able to lose eighty pounds in a little over a year with no other dietary change. I barely recognized her the next time I saw her. She looked fabulous!

A Winning Combination

By combining small amounts of high-glycemic foods such as bread, pasta and potatoes with balanced portions of proteins and fats, you will create a much lower glycemic effect than if you were to eat just the bread, pasta or potatoes by themselves. How you prepare your food also matters a lot. For example, instant oatmeal has almost double the glycemic index of regular slow-cooked oatmeal. Refried beans have a much higher glycemic index than regular beans.

Processing breads, pasta and cereals usually creates a much higher glycemic index. Choose foods that are processed the least or choose unprocessed foods. They usually have a significantly lower glycemic index. Corn and potatoes are fed to pigs and cattle to fatten them up for market. They may have the same effect on you!

Long-Term Consequences

Level 1

If you continue to eat high-glycemic foods, you may eventually become resistant to your body's insulin. This happens when the cells of organs, such as the liver and muscles, are exposed to too much insulin for too long a period of time. These cells begin to close their receptor sites to insulin. Cells of the brain are usually the first to become insulin resistant. In the first stages of insulin resistance you may become increasingly irritable, light-headed and unable to concentrate. This usually occurs a couple of hours after eating a meal packed with carbohydrates, such as pasta, potatoes, bread, rice or high-sugar foods such as cake, cookies and sodas.

Level 2

If you continue keeping your blood sugar level high, it can lead to a second stage of insulin resistance at which the symptoms become more severe. A craving for sugar usually occurs at this stage, as well as weight gain.

If you still do not change your diet, your cells will become increasingly insulin resistant. Your liver will begin to convert excess blood sugar into fat to be stored in the fatty tissues. High insulin levels together with high sugar levels trigger tremendous fat storage. Your body will become a fat-storing dynamo!

> *He gives food to every living thing. His faithful love endures forever. Give thanks to the God of heaven. His faithful love endures forever.*
> —PSALM 136:25–26

Level 3

In the third stage of insulin resistance you will gain weight even more easily, and your craving for

21

starches and sugars will become uncontrollable. Individuals at this third stage are very irritable, tired, depressed and spacey. Often such people take antidepressants, thinking to relieve emotional symptoms when sugar is the problem. By learning to change your diet by eliminating sugars and switching to low-glycemic carbohydrates that are balanced with fats, proteins and fiber, all these symptoms will go away over time.

However, if you continue to eat high-sugar foods, the impact upon your body can be devastating—and permanent if your eating habits do not change.

Final level—diabetes

The final stage of insulin resistance occurs when your body actually shuts down to insulin. During this stage you develop elevated blood sugar and may lose a little weight. At this level the fat cells are usually resistant to insulin, so they shut down, leaving the insulin, blood fat and blood sugar with nowhere to go. The blood sugar is not able to enter the tissues or to be converted and stored as fat. Thus the blood sugar and blood fats are elevated. It is during this fourth stage of insulin resistance that you develop adult-onset diabetes.

The incidence of diabetes in the United States is rising. Diabetes is now the seventh-leading cause of death in the United States. In fact, the number of diabetics is increasing at such a high rate that at the current rate of increase, which is about 6 percent a year, the number of diabetics in this country will double approximately every fifteen years. If you are facing diabetes, let me encourage you to read my book on this topic, *The Bible Cure for Diabetes*.

Excess insulin can lead to obesity in diabetics. It also can lead to hypertension (high blood pressure), elevated cholesterol, elevated triglycerides and heart disease. Too much insulin may also cause your kidneys to retain salt and fluid. It can even cause the muscular layer of arterial walls to grow, making them thicker. High insulin levels may raise levels of norepinephrine, a chemical that constricts blood vessels and increases the heart rate. High insulin levels increase the production of LDL cholesterol (bad cholesterol) and raises blood triglycerides (fats). This in turn may lead to arteriosclerosis of the coronary arteries, which can eventually result in coronary artery disease and heart attacks.

If your diet is keeping your blood sugar levels high, you are flirting with disaster. The consequences are much graver than mere obesity. Diabetes and heart disease are killers. As a doctor, I've watched too many patients suffer the painful destruction to their bodies that comes with these diseases. The saddest part is that it's needless pain and suffering. The power to prevent their pain was in their own hands, but they didn't know it until it was too late.

If you see yourself in these symptoms, don't wait. Make a decision to stop the process of disease in your body right now. God will help you to stay with it if you give Him an opportunity. Why not turn this entire matter over to Him right now?

> *And the LORD God planted all sorts of trees in the garden—beautiful trees that produced delicious fruit. At the center of the garden he placed the tree of life and the tree of the knowledge of good and evil.*
> —GENESIS 2:9

God is at your side to help you. He promises, "I will never leave you nor forsake you" (Heb. 13:5, NKJV). God is your helper and loves you more than you will ever know. He longs to give you all the strength, power and hope you need to triumph in your battle. Pray this Bible Cure prayer and keep pressing forward.

A BIBLE CURE PRAYER
FOR YOU

Lord God, You alone are my strength and my source. My ability to stay committed to weight loss and healthy eating comes from You. Help me to maintain the will power I need to eliminate sugar and empty calories from my diet. Give me the focus I need to implement all that I am learning. Almighty God, replace any discouragement with hope and any doubt with faith. I know that You are with me and will not leave me. I thank You, Lord, for seeing me through this battle and giving me victory over obesity. Amen.

A BIBLE CURE PRESCRIPTION

How many times a day do you eat sugars and carbohydrates?

_____

_____

Describe how you will reduce that frequency.

_____

_____

List the foods high in sugar and starch that you need to eliminate from your diet:

_____

_____

What foods high in protein and fiber have you added to your diet to balance the high-glycemic foods?

_____

_____

_____

Chapter 2

Power for Change
Through Diet and Nutrition

Would you like a supernatural guarantee for success? Here it is: The Bible says to commit your plans to the Lord. "Commit your work to the Lord, and then your plans will succeed" (Prov. 16:3). So I want to encourage you to study this plan and then commit it to the Lord for the strength and will power to follow through.

God is greater than any bondage you may have. And He promises to help you succeed, not with your own power, but by asking for His. He is so faithful. When you ask Him for help, He promises never to fail you or leave you struggling all alone. For the Word of God says, "For God has said, 'I will never fail you. I will never forsake you'" (Heb. 13:5). What a powerful promise!

Let's take a look at a powerful nutritional lifestyle that can help you to discover a healthier, happier, more attractive you.

Stay in Focus

Don't focus on losing weight. Focus instead on eating right. When you eliminate sugar, sweets, excessive carbohydrates, bad fats and yeast from your diet, you will begin to lose weight.

The Bible Cure Fat-Burning, Muscle Building Plan is more than a diet. It is a lifestyle that will help you to look and feel your very best. So, let's get started.

Bible Cure Fat-Burning, Muscle Building Plan

To start, you must first determine your own protein needs. Hold out your hand and look at your palm. How much protein you need each meal can be judged by the size of your palm. Your protein at any one meal should be about the amount that would fit easily in the palm of your hand.

Your Protein Needs

Men should take in approximately 4 ounces of meat with each meal. Women should consume about 3 ounces of meat with each meal.

If you'd like to get a little more technical than the hand-cupping method, you can have your percent of body fat measured by your physician or at a health club to determine your

lean body mass. Many department stores even have percent body fat machines. Calculating your percent of body fat should include your lean body mass. Most percent body fat machines include this in their calculations.

If your physical activity level is moderate, every pound of your lean body mass needs at least 0.6 grams of protein every day.

Keeping It Simple

To keep matters simple, just remember that men will need about 4 ounces of protein with each meal and 1 ounce of protein with each snack.

Women will need 3 ounces of protein with each meal and 1 ounce of protein with each snack.

Adding Carbohydrates

Adding carbohydrates to the protein framework is really quite simple. Let's first look at how to figure out what carbohydrates are in your starchy vegetables. You may have one carbohydrate per meal. (Measurements are after the vegetable has been cooked—not before cooking.)

A MAN EATING 4 OZ. MEAT MAY EAT:	A WOMAN EATING 3 OZ. MEAT MAY EAT:
1 c. pasta	¾ c. pasta
1 c. corn	¾ c. corn
1 c. lima beans	¾ c. lima beans
1 c. refried beans	¾ c. refried beans
¾ c. rice	½ c. rice
¾ c. mashed potatoes	½ c. mashed potatoes
1⅓ c. peas	1 c. peas
1⅓ c. pinto beans	1 c. pinto beans
1⅓ c. baked potatoes	1 c. baked potatoes
1⅓ c. sweet potatoes	1 c. sweet potatoes
1⅓ c. oatmeal	1 c. oatmeal
1⅓ c. grits	1 c. grits
2 8-in. tortillas	1½ 8-in. tortillas
2 4-in. pancakes	1½ 4-in. pancakes

Hopefully you are getting the idea that you can't eat a whole lot of starchy foods on the Bible Cure program if you desire to lose weight.

As you've already learned, proteins must be

properly balanced with carbohydrates so as not to cause a rise in insulin.

Bread

A man would need approximately two slices or less of whole-grain bread with the 4 ounces of protein at a meal. A woman will only need about one and one-half slices of whole grain bread with her 3 ounces of protein. Or to make matters simple, she can just trim the crust from around the edges.

Now for the Vegetables

Now, let's take a look at the vegetables that can be combined with proteins. You do not have to eat just one vegetable or one starch. You may eat half of your starch allotment and fill in the remainder with vegetables.

Cooked vegetables. If a typical man eats 4 ounces of protein with one meal, to balance the protein with carbohydrates he can eat 4 cups of the following cooked vegetables. A woman may eat 3 cups (or ½ of a starch and 1½ cups of one of the following):

- Broccoli
- Asparagus

- Green beans
- Brussels sprouts
- Collard greens
- Okra, spinach
- Turnips
- Zucchini
- Squash

Raw vegetables. A man may eat 8 cups while a woman may have 6. (It is doubtful that an individual would desire this much food. However, this shows the maximum amount of vegetables a person may eat compared to starch. It is possible to have ½ of the starch and fill the remainder with vegetables and fruits.)

- Broccoli
- Cabbage
- Cauliflower
- Celery
- Radishes

Both men and women may eat:

- 4 heads of lettuce
- 16 c. spinach
- 24 c. romaine lettuce
- 8 tomatoes

You do not have to remember all of these figures. You can simply eat as much salad, iceberg lettuce, spinach or romaine lettuce as you want with mushrooms, onions, tomatoes, radishes, peppers, cucumbers, cauliflower, broccoli and sprouts.

Fruits

Now let's take a look at the fruits.

A MAN EATING 4 OZ. MEAT MAY EAT:	A WOMAN EATING 3 OZ. MEAT MAY EAT:
4 c. cubed cantaloupe	3 c. cubed cantaloupe
4 c. strawberries	3 c. strawberries
2 c. honeydew	1½ c. honeydew
2 c. watermelon	1½ c. watermelon
2 c. pineapple	1½ c. pineapple
2 c. peaches	1½ c. peaches
2 c. blackberries	1½ c. blackberries
2 c. blueberries	1½ c. blueberries
2 c. grapes	1½ c. grapes
2 grapefruits	1½ grapefruits
2 apples	1½ apples
2 oranges	1½ oranges
4 plums	3 plums
4 tangerines	3 tangerines

It is very simple to see that if you eat vegetables and fruits, you can eat almost as much as you desire, adding them to your 4 ounces of protein (or 3 ounces for women) and being totally satisfied.

It's best to choose vegetables and fruits for your carbohydrates if you desire to lose weight rapidly. To lose weight even faster, choose only vegetables and salads for the carbohydrates, and eat starches and fruits very sparingly.

Fat

The last ingredient that we must add is the fat. Yes, you must take in fat to burn fat. However, it is best to choose foods that are rich in monounsaturated fats. These include the following (men and women may eat the same amount):

- Olive oil, 1–2 tsp. on salad
- Natural peanut butter, 1–2 tsp.
- Almond butter, 2 tsp.
- Avocado, 2 Tbsp.
- Organic butter, 1 tsp.
- Sour cream, 2 Tbsp.
- Cream cheese, 1 Tbsp.

I also use 1–2 teaspoons of canola mayonnaise, which I get from the health food store. Other good fats include:

- Cold-pressed safflower oil, 1–2 tsp.
- Cold-pressed sunflower oil or sesame oil, 1–2 tsp.
- Cold-pressed canola oil, 1–2 tsp.

If you have olive oil and vinegar dressing, men and women can use 4 teaspoons.

Following are nuts that you can eat:

- Peanuts, 2–4
- Macadamia nuts, 4
- Almond slivers, 4 tsp.
- Walnuts (chopped), 2 tsp.

A BIBLE CURE HEALTH TIP

Avoid Hydrogenated and Partially Hydrogenated Fats!

Hydrogenated fat is prepared by taking polyunsaturated fat such as corn oil, heating it to a high temperature and using high pressure to force hydrogen through it until it is saturated. This process permanently alters the structure of the fat and forms an unnatural configuration called *trans-configuration*.

Trans fatty acids are found in margarine and in most processed foods, including baked goods, pastries, cookies, cakes, pies, breads, many salad dressings, mayonnaise and many other foods. Read labels carefully, and avoid foods that contain hydrogenated or partially hydrogenated fats.

Snacks

To make things simple, many health foods stores carry forty-thirty-thirty bars and forty-thirty-thirty protein mixes so that you may have a snack or even a meal that is perfectly balanced. They contain 40 percent carbohydrates, 30 percent protein and 30 percent fat. These allow you to be satisfied, have tremendous energy and burn fat at the same time.

A Simple Rule of Thumb

Men should have about 4 ounces of protein with each meal and 1 ounce of protein as a snack. A woman should have 3 ounces of protein with a meal and ¾ ounces as a snack.

Simply choose a 4-ounce piece of chicken breast, turkey breast, fish or lean red meat and balance this with all the salad, vegetables and fruit that you want.

Some people are unable to eat fruit with protein because it causes tremendous gas. If this happens to you, simply eat fruit with vegetable protein such as soy to prevent gas and bloating.

Remember to add a small amount of fat as listed above.

Beware of Fad Diets!

Many high-carbohydrate diets are too low in protein. Thus, muscle tone is lost, and weight is gained easily. You should eat protein with each meal and every snack!

Planning Your Menus

Now, I would like to help you plan a week of menus.

DAY ONE

BREAKFAST	
<u>MEN</u>	<u>WOMEN</u>
• 1 c. old-fashioned oatmeal	• ¾ c. oatmeal
• ½ c. skim milk	• ⅓ c. cottage cheese
• 2 tsp. walnuts	• 2 tsp. walnuts
• 1 tsp. honey	• ¾ tsp. honey
• ½ c. cottage cheese	

LUNCH	
<u>MEN</u>	<u>WOMEN</u>
• 4 oz. chicken breast	• 3 oz. chicken
• 1 tsp. canola mayonnaise	• 1 tsp. canola mayonnaise
• Lettuce	• Lettuce
• Tomato slice	

- 2 slices whole-grain bread
- A large spinach salad with 1 Tbsp. low-fat, sugar-free dressing

- Tomato slice
- 1½ slice whole-grain bread (or trim crust)
- A large spinach salad with 1 Tbsp. low-fat, sugar-free dressing

MIDAFTERNOON SNACK

A forty-thirty-thirty bar

DINNER

MEN
- 4 oz. salmon
- Salad with peppers, onions, mushrooms, celery, cucumber and sprouts
- 1 Tbsp. low-fat, sugar-free dressing
- ½ cup fruit cocktail

WOMEN
- 3 oz. salmon
- Salad with peppers, onions, mushrooms, celery, cucumber and sprouts
- 1 Tbsp. low-fat, sugar-free dressing
- ⅓ cup fruit cocktail

A BIBLE CURE HEALTH TIP

Enjoy Oatmeal!

Gamma-linolenic acid (GLA) is another important fatty acid in the production of good eicosanoids. Eicosanoids regulate blood pressure, blood clotting, the immune system, inflammatory response, pain and fever responses, constriction and dilation of blood vessels, constriction and dialation of airways and lungs, release of gastric acis, and they effect almost every other bodily function. However, for GLA to produce good eicosanoids, you must decrease or avoid sugar and high-glycemic foods or balance them with the correct amounts of protein and fat. You can easily get adequate GLA in your diet by eating cooked oatmeal every other day or by taking one gelcap of borage oil (available at a health food store) three times a week. Avoid instant oatmeal, however. It is too high in carbohydrates.

DAY TWO

BREAKFAST

MEN	WOMEN
• ¾ c. low-fat cottage cheese	• ½ c. low-fat cottage cheese
• 2 c. peaches	• 1 c. peaches
• 1 Tbsp. slivered almonds	• ½ Tbsp. slivered almonds

LUNCH

MEN	WOMEN
• 4 oz. water-packed tuna, preferably albacore	• 3 oz. tuna, preferably albacore
• 1 tsp. canola mayonnaise	• 1 tsp. canola mayonnaise
• Chopped celery, chopped onions, lettuce, tomato	• Chopped celery, chopped onions, lettuce, tomato
• 2 slices whole-grain bread	• 1½ slices whole-grain bread

Forty-thirty-thirty protein shake or supplement

DINNER

MEN
- 4 oz. turkey
- 1 c. steamed broccoli spears
- ½ baked potato with a pat of butter

WOMEN
- 3 oz. turkey
- 1 c. steamed broccoli spears
- ⅓ baked potato

A BIBLE CURE HEALTHFACT

Protein is critically important for rebuilding and repairing the body and for maintaining our immune system. When you eat high-protein foods such as chicken, fish and turkey, protein is broken down into amino acids in your body. These amino acids are absorbed and used as building blocks in forming thousands of different proteins, which are essential throughout the body. Some of the proteins are used for the immune system and in forming muscle, hormones, enzymes and neurotransmitters.

HEALTHFACT HEALTHFACT HEALTHFACT HEALTHFACT HEALTHFACT HEALTHFACT HEALTHFACT

DAY THREE

BREAKFAST

MEN
- 1 whole egg and 2 eggs whites, scrambled

WOMEN
- 1 whole egg and 1 egg white, scrambled

- 1 oz. low-fat cheddar cheese
- Chopped onion and chopped tomatoes scrambled with eggs
- 2 slices whole-grain toast
- Pat of butter
- ½ c. orange juice

- 1 oz. low-fat cheddar cheese
- Chopped onion and chopped tomatoes scrambled with eggs
- 1 slice whole-grain toast
- Pat of butter
- ½ c. orange juice

LUNCH

MEN
- Chicken fajitas with 4 oz. chicken strips
- 2 8-in. flour tortillas
- 2 Tbsp. guacamole
- ½ c. salsa
- Chopped lettuce

WOMEN
- Chicken fajitas with 3 oz. chicken strips
- 1½ tortillas
- 2 Tbsp. guacamole
- ¼ c. salsa
- Chopped lettuce

MIDAFTERNOON SNACK

MEN
- 4 oz. cottage cheese
- 1 c. strawberries

WOMEN
- 3 oz. cottage cheese
- ¾ c. strawberries

DINNER

MEN
- 4 oz. lean filet mignon, preferably free-range meat
- ½ baked potato
- Pat of butter
- 1 c. steamed asparagus
- Large salad with low-fat, sugar-free salad dressing

WOMEN
- 3 oz. lean filet mignon
- ⅓ baked potato
- Pat of butter
- 1 c. steamed asparagus
- Large salad with low-fat, sugar-free salad dressing

DAY FOUR

BREAKFAST

MEN
- 1½ scoops whey protein
  (17.5 gr. protein per scoop)
- 1 c. frozen strawberries
- ½ c. frozen peaches
- 1 c. water
- 1 Tbsp. walnuts or almonds
- 1 tsp. honey

WOMEN
- 1 scoop whey protein

- ¾ c. strawberries
- ⅓ c. frozen peaches
- 1 c. water
- 1 Tbsp. walnuts
  or almonds

Blend together until smooth.

LUNCH

MEN
- 4 oz. roast beef
- 2 slices whole-grain bread
- 1 tsp. mayonnaise
- 1 tsp. mustard
- Lettuce leaf and a slice
  of tomato

WOMEN
- 3 oz. roast beef
- 1½ slices whole-grain
  bread
- 1 tsp. mayonnaise
- 1 tsp. mustard
- Lettuce leaf and a slice
  of tomato

MIDAFTERNOON SNACK

MEN
- 1 scoop soy protein powder
  (approx. 15 gr. of protein)
- ½ frozen banana
- ½ tsp. natural peanut butter
- ⅔ c. water

WOMEN
- ½ scoop soy protein
  powder
- ⅓ frozen banana
- ½ tsp. natural peanut
  butter
- ⅔ c. water

Blend until smooth, sweetening with Stevia, which is available
from a health food store.

MEN
- Chili, with 4 oz. lean ground beef, preferably free-range
- Shredded low-fat cheese
- ½ c. kidney beans with chili powder
- 1 c. sliced tomatoes
- ⅓ c. chopped onions
- 1 tsp. olive oil

WOMEN
- Chili, with 3 oz. lean ground beef, preferably free-range
- Shredded low-fat cheese
- ⅓ c. kidney beans with chili powder
- ¾ c. sliced tomatoes
- ¼ c. chopped onions
- 1 tsp. olive oil

DAY FIVE

BREAKFAST

MEN
- 1 c. plain low-fat yogurt
- ½ c. peaches mixed with the yogurt
- 4 links soy sausage
- ½ slice whole-grain toast
- 1 Tbsp. almond butter

WOMEN
- ¾ c. plain low-fat yogurt
- ⅓ c. peaches mixed with yogurt
- 3 links soy sausage
- 1 Tbsp. almond butter

LUNCH

MEN
- Chicken salad sandwich with 4 oz. shredded chicken breast
- 2 slices whole-grain bread
- 1 tsp. canola mayonnaise
- Slice of tomato, leaf of lettuce, a small amount chopped celery

WOMEN
- Chicken salad sandwich with 3 oz. shredded chicken breast
- 1½ slices of whole-grain bread
- 1 tsp. canola mayonnaise
- Slice of tomato, leaf of lettuce, a small amount chopped celery

1 oz. low-fat cheese with half an apple

DINNER

MEN
- 4 oz. chicken
- 1 c. pasta
- Dinner salad with tomatoes, onions, cucumbers, celery
- 1⅓ Tbsp. olive oil and vinegar dressing

WOMEN
- 3 oz. chicken
- ¾ cup pasta
- Dinner salad with tomatoes, onions, cucumbers, celery
- 1⅓ Tbsp. olive oil and vinegar dressing

A BIBLE CURE HEALTH TIP

Eat Cold-Water Fish

Choose fish oil, which is an Omega-3 fatty acid found in cold-water fish such as salmon, mackerel, herring or halibut. You can eat cold-water fish several times a week or take one to two fish oil capsules with each meal. However, make sure that the fish oil has undergone molecular distillation in order to remove toxins and heavy metals.

DAY SIX

BREAKFAST

MEN
- 1 whole egg and 2 eggs whites
- 2 oz. soy bacon or 4 links soy sausage

WOMEN
- 1 whole egg and 1 egg white
- 1½ oz. soy bacon or

44

- 1⅓ c. cooked grits with 1–2 pats of butter

3 links soy sausage
- 1 c. cooked grits with 1–2 pats of butter

LUNCH

MEN
- 4 oz. lean hamburger, preferably free-range
- 2 slices whole-grain bread
- A slice of tomato, 1 lettuce leaf, 1 onion slice
- 1 tsp. canola mayonnaise
- 1 tsp. mustard

WOMEN
- 3 oz. lean hamburger preferably free-range
- 1½ slices whole-grain bread
- A slice of tomato, 1 lettuce leaf, 1 onion slice
- 1 tsp. canola mayonnaise
- 1 tsp. mustard

MIDAFTERNOON SNACK

Forty-thirty-thirty supplement bar or protein drink

DINNER

MEN
- ⅔ c. cooked pasta (spaghetti)
- 4 oz. lean red meat, preferably free-range, to add to spaghetti sauce, which should also contain at least 1 tsp. extra-virgin olive oil, garlic, onions, mushrooms and tomatoes

WOMEN
- ½ c. cooked pasta (spaghetti)
- 3 oz. lean, red meat, preferably free-range, to add to spaghetti sauce, which should also contain at least 1 tsp. extra-virgin olive oil, garlic, onions, mushrooms and tomatoes

DAY SEVEN

BREAKFAST

MEN
- 1 whole-grain bagel
- 1 Tbsp. low-fat cream cheese
- 4 oz. turkey breast on the bagel

WOMEN
- ¾ whole-grain bagel
- 1 Tbsp. low-fat cream cheese
- 3 oz. turkey breast on the bagel

LUNCH

MEN
- 4 oz. lean roast beef, preferably free-range
- 1 lettuce leaf, 1 tomato slice
- 1 tsp. mustard
- 1 tsp. canola mayonnaise
- 2 slices whole-grain bread

WOMEN
- 3 oz. lean roast beef, preferably free-range
  1 lettuce leaf, 1 tomato slice
- 1 tsp. mustard
- 1 tsp. canola mayonnaise
- 1½ slices whole-grain bread

MIDAFTERNOON SNACK

Forty-thirty-thirty supplement bar or protein drink

DINNER

MEN
- Chicken Caesar salad with ½ head romaine lettuce, 4 oz. grilled chicken breast
- ½ oz. croutons
- 1 Tbsp. grated Parmesan cheese
- 2 tsp. Caesar salad dressing

WOMEN
- Chicken Caesar salad with ½ head romaine lettuce, 3 oz. grilled chicken breast
- 1 Tbsp. grated Parmesan cheese
- 2 tsp. Caesar salad dressing

Attempt to eat at least four to five times a day with three meals and one to two snack breaks. The snacks should be in the midafternoon. One may occasionally need a bedtime snack similar to the midafternoon snack. Drink approximately 8 ounces of water thirty minutes before each meal, and limit fluids to only 4 ounces with a meal. You may drink water with lemon or tea with lemon, sweetened with Stevia (available from a health food store) and not sugar. However, avoid sodas, fruit juices and other high-sugar beverages. Try to drink at least two quarts of filtered water a day. You must have adequate water to flush the fat from your body.

Avoid NutraSweet since it breaks down into methyl alcohol and formaldehyde in your body. Don't go longer than five hours without eating. I recommend that you carry a forty-thirty-thirty supplement bar with you so that your blood sugar level doesn't drop and trigger carbohydrate or sugar cravings.

Now that you have your plan, success is only a matter of time. Here are some additional eating tips that will help you along the way.

Eating Tips

1. Eat the protein portion of your meal first since this stimulates glucagon, which will depress insulin secretion and cause the release of carbohydrates that have been stored in the liver and muscles, which will help prevent low blood sugar.

2. Chew each bite at least twenty to thirty times and eat slowly.

3. Never rush through a meal. Rushing will cause hydrochloric acid to be suppressed, making digestion difficult.

4. Never eat when you are upset, angry or bickering. Eating should be a time of relaxation.

5. Limit your starches to only one serving per meal. Never eat bread, pasta, potatoes, corn and different starches together at one meal. This elevates insulin levels. If you do go back for seconds, choose fruits and vegetables and salads, but not starches.

6. If you are craving a dessert, simply eliminate the starch or the bread, pasta, potatoes and corn and have a small dessert. However, be sure to have

your protein and fat to balance out the sugar in the dessert. Also, don't eat desserts regularly. Only do this on special occasions such as birthdays, holidays and anniversaries.

7. Avoid alcoholic beverages, not only because alcohol is toxic to our bodies, but also because it triggers a tremendous insulin release and promotes storage of fat.

Eating Out

You can eat out and still enjoy a balanced Bible Cure Program meal. Again, simply choose 3 to 4 ounces of lean meat and balance this out with fats and carbohydrates, which include fruits, vegetables or starches. For example, at a steak restaurant you can have 4 ounces of lean filet mignon (3 ounces for a woman), a small baked potato with a pat of butter (½ baked potato for a woman) and a salad with 1 tablespoon of low-fat, sugar-free salad dressing.

Here are some additional tips for eating out.

Eating out at specialty food restaurants
Mexican. Men should choose the chicken

fajitas with 2 tortillas, 4 ounces chicken, 1–2 tablespoons of guacamole or sour cream, salsa and lettuce. Women should have 3 ounces chicken with 1½ tortillas. However, do not choose rice or beans.

Italian. Men should choose 4 ounces grilled chicken breast or chicken Marsala with 1 cup pasta. Women should choose 3 ounces of meat with ¾ cup pasta. The Marsala sauce has plenty of olive oil in to provide your fats.

Chinese. Men can choose ¾ cup white rice and stir-fried chicken (4 ounces) with Chinese vegetables. Women can have ½ cup white rice with 3 ounces of stir-fried chicken. Make sure that they do not put excessive amounts of sesame seed oil in your stir-fry. It is best not to pour the sauce on top of the rice but to pick the chicken and vegetables out of the sauce and combine it with the rice.

Japanese. Men can eat approximately ¾ cup rice with Japanese vegetables and 4 ounces of chicken, shrimp or lean beef, along with the house salad with ginger dressing. Women can eat ½ cup rice with 3 ounces of meat.

Fast foods. Choose the salad bar and have a grilled chicken sandwich with only one piece of the bun (or no bun at all). You may also have an occasional hamburger with mustard, but not ketchup, and only one piece of the bun (or no bun at all). Add lettuce and tomatoes and take a piece of the bun off. Avoid the soft drinks, French fries and apple pies.

A Final Word

Almost everyone will eventually eat the wrong foods in the wrong combinations, so don't feel condemned when this happens; simply get back on track and start combining your foods correctly.

This is not a diet, but a lifestyle. So follow this lifestyle every day. There will be times that you will slip, especially on holidays, birthdays, anniversaries, weddings and other special occasions. However, never give up. Simply get back on the program, and you will again start burning fat and building muscle.

If you reach a plateau or if you are unable to lose more weight, simply avoid high-glycemic carbohydrates, which include breads, pasta, potatoes, corn, rice, pretzels, bagels, crackers, cereals, popcorn, beans, bananas and dried fruit. Choose low-glycemic vegetables and fruits. If after a month or two of doing this you are still unable to lose sufficient weight, you should choose low-glycemic vegetables and salads and avoid fruits for approximately a month until you break through the plateau. Then reintroduce low-glycemic fruits.

I am praying for God to give you the determination and will power to follow through on this eating strategy. Not only will you lose weight, but you will keep it off. In doing so, you will take care of your body,

> *Listen to my prayer for mercy as I cry out to you for help, as I lift my hands toward your holy sanctuary.*
> —PSALM 28:2

God's temple, and live a full and abundant life to His glory. Eat right and walk in divine health!

A BIBLE CURE PRAYER
FOR YOU

Lord, give me the will and determination to eat right and lose weight. Break the bondage of obesity in my life that keeps me from enjoying an abundant life in Christ. Let me be filled with Your strength and power to follow a healthy lifestyle and eat the right foods so that I may serve and love You with my whole heart. Amen.

Keep a Daily Food Diary

Date/ Weight	Breakfast	Lunch	Dinner
/			
/			
/			
/			
/			
/			
/			
/			
/			

Make copies as needed

The body mass index is simply a formula that considers your weight and height to determine if you are healthy, overweight or obese. Overweight is defined as a body mass index of 25 to 29. Obesity is defined as a body mass index of 30 or more. Find your own body mass index on the chart below by drawing a line from your weight (left column) to your height (right column). Is your BMI (middle column) in the "healthy" range?

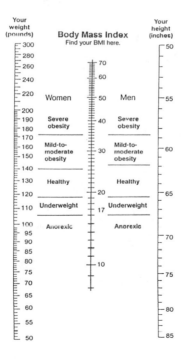

Chapter 3

Power for
Change Through Exercise

God has made you the master of your body—it is not the master of you! Too many of us let our bodies tell us what to do. However, God created this incredible machine to be your servant. The apostle Paul revealed his understanding of this truth when he said, "I discipline my body like an athlete, training it to do what it should. Otherwise, I fear that after preaching to others I myself might be disqualified" (1 Cor. 9:27).

God has given you the power of mastery over your body. If you've let it get out of shape, it's time to assert your power!

Proper nutrition alone cannot reduce your weight sufficiently or adequately maintain your proper weight. However, proper nutrition combined with exercise will help you reach your goal of walking in divine health and living a long, wholesome life.

Exercise Regularly

Exercise is extremely important if you want to lose weight and keep it off. Aerobic exercise uses large muscle groups of the body and raises the heart rate to a range that will burn fat for fuel. As a result, aerobic exercise is one of the best ways to lose body fat. Aerobic exercise includes brisk walking, cycling, swimming, rowing, skiing and dancing.

It's important to see your personal physician before starting a rigorous exercise program.

Try brisk walking. Brisk walking is the simplest and most convenient way to exercise aerobically. You should walk briskly enough so that you can't sing, yet slow enough so that you can talk. Aerobic exercise will make you feel better immediately by putting more oxygen into your body.

Aerobic exercise also tones the heart and blood vessels, increases circulation, boosts the metabolic rate, improves digestion and elimination, controls insulin production, stimulates the production of neurotransmitters in the brain, improves the appetite and stimulates the lymphatic system, which aids in the removal of toxic material from the body.

One of the best ways to know if you are getting enough aerobic exercise is to monitor your heart rate. You should be exercising vigorously enough

> *For God has not given us a spirit of fear and timidity, but of power, love, and self-discipline.*
> —2 TIMOTHY 1:7

to raise your heart rate to at least a 65 to 80 percent level of your predicted maximum heart rate. (Please see my book *The Bible Cure for Diabetes* for instructions on how to calculate your predicted heart rate.)

High-intensity aerobic exercise actually decreases insulin levels and increases levels of glucagon. By lowering insulin levels, you begin to release more stored body fat, and thus you burn fat, not carbohydrates. I recommend that you exercise at close to 80 percent of your predicted maximum heart rate in order to reduce insulin levels, increase glucagon and burn more fat.

☑ A BIBLE CURE HEALTHFACT

Have you thought that having a high metabolism was others' blessing, but not yours? It's not.

Your metabolic rate is dependent upon your muscle mass. The more muscle mass you have, the higher your metabolic rate. If your dieting efforts do not include exercise, you can begin to burn muscle mass to supply your body with amino acids and sabotage your weight-loss efforts by slowing down your metabolic rate. The body will then begin to burn fewer calories and less fat. The more muscle you carry, the higher the metabolic rate and the more stored body fat you will burn—even at rest.

HealthFact HealthFact HealthFact HealthFact HealthFact HealthFact HealthFact

Also use anaerobic exercise. Anaerobic exercise such as weightlifting, sprinting and resistance training will help to increase lean muscle mass—thereby increasing your metabolic rate. If the workout is intense enough, growth hormone will be released from the pituitary gland. This leads to increased muscle growth and increased fat loss.

For maximum results, however, the exercise must be very strenuous and done until muscle exhaustion occurs or until you simply cannot move any more. This stimulates the release of a powerful surge of growth hormone, which helps to repair and rebuild the muscles that have been broken down during the workout. As you gain more muscle mass, your metabolic rate rises.

A word of caution, however: If you weigh

yourself, the scale may not show a dramatic weight loss since the muscle mass that you are adding actually weighs more than the fat it is replacing.

If you are just beginning a weightlifting program, I recommend that you consult a certified personal trainer who will develop a well-rounded weightlifting program for you. As you exercise, be sure to maintain proper form and lift the weights slowly to avoid injury.

Increased sugar and increased starch will inhibit growth hormone release and is counterproductive. Therefore, prior to a workout, avoid snacks that are high in sugar or carbohy-

> *He renews my strength. He guides me along right paths, bringing honor to his name.*
> —PSALM 23:3

drates since you will not have the advantage of this powerful hormone for fat loss and muscle gain.

The Importance of Sleep

Another way to stimulate release of growth hormone is to be sure that you get a good night's sleep. Growth hormone is secreted during stage three and stage four sleep, which occurs during the first couple of hours after falling asleep.

Hitting a Plateau

If you lose weight steadily and then seem to hit a plateau, exercise will help. By increasing the frequency and duration of exercise, you can break through that plateau and continue losing weight. Try to increase your exercise time gradually from twenty minutes to forty-five minutes. Just add five additional minutes of exercise each week until you reach forty-five minutes. Those stubborn last few pounds will soon begin to melt away.

Stewarding the Gift of Your Body

Your body is a wonderful gift. With God's help, you can get back into shape, feel better and look fabulous. Determine right now to put these exercise tips into practice and, most importantly, to stay with it. Remember, everyone falls down, but it takes an individual with courage to get back up again. You will have your ups and downs—we all do. But hang in there. Stay with it. Before long, you'll look like the person you've always dreamed of becoming!

61

A BIBLE CURE PRAYER
FOR YOU

Lord, I surrender all my cares to You. Give me the power of a disciplined life. Thank You for the gift of my body. I realize that it is a temple of the Holy Spirit and I must be a good steward of it. Each time I become discouraged or want to quit, please be there to pick me up and put me back on track. I surrender the care of my body to you and your wonderful wisdom. In the name of Jesus Christ, amen.

A BIBLE CURE PRESCRIPTION

Check the lifestyle changes you are willing to make to achieve weight loss:

❑ Exercise regularly. The type of exercise you
   will get is: _____
❑ Get enough sleep.
❑ Begin an aerobic program.
❑ Other: _____

Write a prayer asking God for help in making these lifestyle changes.

_____

_____

_____

Write a prayer of commitment asking God for His help in staying faithful to an exercise program.

_____

_____

_____

Chapter 4

Power for Change Through Vitamins and Supplements

Your body is the temple of God's Spirit. The apostle Paul writes, "Don't you know that your body is the temple of the Holy Spirit, who lives in you and was given to you by God? You do not belong to yourself, for God bought you with a high price. So you must honor God with your body" (1 Cor. 6:19–20).

Your body is also the most incredible natural machine in the entire universe. All the money in the world could not replace it. It's God's awesome gift and a suitable place to house His own Spirit. Since your body was created as the temple of God's Spirit, it's important to understand that you and I are merely stewards of this gift God has given us.

If you went out today and purchased a Mercedes-Benz or a Porsche, no doubt you would polish it and fill it with the best gas, the best oil—treating it with the respect that such a fine machine deserves. You can honor God in your body as well by treating it with the respect and care that befits such a wonderful gift.

By giving your body the nutrients, vitamins and minerals it needs to function at peak performance, you will bring honor to God by properly caring for your body—the temple He created on earth to house His own Spirit.

What Is Your Body Trying to Tell You?

Your incredible body is so sophisticated that it is programmed to signal you that it needs a nutrient or a vitamin that you haven't supplied. These signals come in the form of cravings. Have you ever just had to have a glass of orange juice? Your body was telling your brain that it needed some more vitamin C.

Cravings can come following a meal when the body realizes that, although it's been fed, it still hasn't received enough of the nutrients it expected. Too often, instead of discerning the craving properly, we simply fuel our bodies with even more non-nutritious food. Therefore, the cravings return, and we respond once again with more junk food. The cycle becomes vicious, we get fatter and our bodies suffer for lack of real nutrition.

If you experience such cravings, it's likely your body is actually slightly malnourished. Vitamins, minerals and supplements are vital in today's world for the proper fueling of our bodies. You see, most old-time farmers know that in order for soil to supply the food it produces with a rich supply of vitamins and minerals, it must rest or lie fallow. In other words, it must remain unused every few years. In today's world of high-tech agriculture, this no longer occurs. Therefore, our food supplies are actually depleted of the vitamins, minerals and nutrients our bodies need to maintain good health. So we give our bodies more and more food, but they still lack vitamins and nutrients. That's where supplementation can bridge the gap.

Natural Substances for You

Let's explore some of these natural substances that can promote health and vitality as you defeat obesity in your life. We will also look at some of the supplements available that you should avoid as you take the necessary steps to reach your ideal weight.

A good multivitamin. It's important to be sure that you get a good supply of all the various vitamins your body needs, especially if it is depleted. Most multivitamins contain only twelve vitamins, and many of them lack vitamin K. When you purchase a vitamin supplement, be sure that it contains vitamin K. You may want to choose a multivitamin you can take two to three times a day.

A good multimineral. Choosing a mineral supplement is a little more difficult than choosing a vitamin supplement and sometimes more costly. Find a mineral supplement that is chelated rather than one that contains mineral salts. Chelation is a process of wrapping a mineral with an organic molecule such as an amino acid that increases absorption dramatically.

A word of caution about colloidal minerals: Many of these have extremely high amounts of aluminum in them. They may also contain mercury, arsenic and other toxic minerals. Therefore, avoid colloidal mineral supplements.

B-complex vitamins. To prevent our adrenal glands from becoming exhausted we need to supplement our diets daily with a comprehensive multivitamin and mineral formula with adequate amounts of B-complex vitamins. Divine Health Multivitamin has vitamins, chelated minerals and antioxidants in a balanced comprehensive formula.

Ginseng can also help support the adrenal glands. Taking 200 milligrams of ginseng two to three times per day will help support the adrenal gland, thus allowing you to handle stress.

DSF Formula is an adrenal glandular supplement by Nutri-West. It is an important aid in helping your body to cope with the effects of stress, which can actually cause you to gain weight. Take ½ to 1 tablet at breakfast and at lunch.

5-HTP. Many overweight individuals are depressed, and I have found that supplements of 5-HTP (5-hydroxytryptophan) in a dose of 50–100 milligrams three times a day with meals will not only help depression but will also promote satiety, thus fewer calories are consumed at meal times. You should not take 5-HTP if you are taking any other antidepressant.

Fiber. Another supplement that I find very effective in promoting weight loss and stabilizing insulin levels is fiber. One teaspoon of soluble fiber such as Perdiem, which is sold over the counter, taken usually five or ten minutes before meals with 8 or 10 ounces of water will make a person feel full. It will also help to control blood sugar and help lower insulin levels.

Other soluble fibers include oat bran and guar gum. Avoid using soluble fibers that contain sugar or NutraSweet.

Garcinia cambogia, otherwise known as hydroxycitric acid, may suppress appetite as well as inhibit the conversion of carbohydrates into fat. The normal dose is 500–1000 milligrams, three times a day. This is usually taken approximately thirty minutes before meals.

Chromium is a mineral that is able to increase the body's sensitivity to insulin. Chromium occurs naturally in our foods, but much of it can be lost when the foods are refined or processed. Therefore, many of our diets are deficient in chromium. Also junk foods, sodas and excessive sugar can deplete us of our chromium stores.

Chromium is a cofactor of insulin. In other words, if your body doesn't have enough chromium, it needs more insulin to do its job. So extra insulin is released whenever high-sugar or high-carbohydrate foods or drinks are consumed. GTF chromium is glucose-tolerance-factor chromium.

However, you should make sure that it is certified biologically active.

Other forms of chromium include chromium picolinate and chromium poly-nicotinate. Picolinate enables chromium to enter readily into the body's cells, where the mineral can then help

> *It is useless for you to work so hard from early morning until late at night, anxiously working for food to eat; for God gives rest to his loved ones.*
> —Psalm 127:2

insulin do its job more effectively. However, tests on this variety have indicated some possible problems, so I recommend choosing another variety to be safe.

Chromium supplementation has been shown to be able to lower body fat yet increase lean body mass. This is probably due to increased insulin sensitivity. The normal dose of chromium is approximately 200–400 micrograms per day.

Use caution with supplements containing ephedrine, caffeine and aspirin. When we go to the health food store we see shelves and shelves of supplements for weight loss. Many of these are thermogenic aids, which include ephedrine, caffeine and aspirin. However, these products can cause high blood pressure and rapid heartbeats. Therefore a doctor should monitor patients on these products. These supplements are very effective for weight loss; however, dangerous side effects may occur in some people. You should be examined by a physician prior to starting these supplements.

Use caution with chitosan. Fat blockers such as chitosan will interfere with the absorption of essential fatty acids and fat-soluble vitamins. Therefore, I do not routinely recommend these supplements, and they should not be taken for a prolonged period of time.

A Lifestyle Choice

Many people hope for a pill or supplement that will miraculously help them lose weight. The truth is that there is no shortcut to losing weight and keeping it off. A new lifestyle that includes good nutrition, exercise, supplementation and constant diligence is the best way to overcome obesity. The vitamins and supplements I have suggested can help you, but only you can decide to begin an entirely new lifestyle filled with health, vitality and God's very best! Make that determination at this very moment.

A Bible Cure Prayer
FOR YOU

Lord, thank You for vitamins and supplements that can help me battle obesity. Help me to be diligent in a plan to overcome obesity and to live a healthy lifestyle guided by Your Spirit and plan for divine health. Amen.

A BIBLE CURE PRESCRIPTION

Check the steps you are willing to take:

- ❑ Take B-complex vitamins
- ❑ Avoid aspirin, caffeine and ephedrine
- ❑ Use fiber
- ❑ Take chromium
- ❑ Other: _____

Describe the diligent ways you are walking in divine health:

_____

_____

_____

_____

_____

_____

_____

_____

_____

_____

Chapter 5

Power for Change
Through Faith in God

Jesus said, "Come to me, all of you who are weary and carry heavy burdens, and I will give your rest. Take my yoke upon you. Let me teach you, because I am humble and gentle, and you will find rest for your souls. For my yoke fits perfectly, and the burden I give you is light" (Matt. 11:28–30).

There is no greater love in the universe than the love God feels for you. No matter what you've done or neglected to do, He loves you more than you could ever know. And He longs to reveal His love to you in every place of emotional need. He tenderly calls you—even at this very moment— asking you to give Him all of the hurts, hidden pain and disappointments that you've been carrying around with you. The Bible instructs,

"Give all your worries and cares to God, for he cares about what happens to you" (1 Pet. 5:7).

Look once again at what He said: "Come to me." How often have you—for lack of comfort, nervousness, because of a numb inability to really face your emotional pain or from a hollow sense of aloneness—opened up the refrigerator and filled an empty place in your heart with a piece of pie or a cupcake?

You see, just as with a drug, food can temporarily anesthetize you from the pain of loneliness, abandonment, fear, stress and emotional pain. It's no wonder the American population is getting larger. We are a nation emotionally hurting from a lack of love. But food cannot truly fill that void—even if we haven't faced it for so long that we hardly notice it anymore.

But I have really good news for you. Jesus Christ can fill it, and He can comfort your heart with a sense of peace that will overwhelm you with true joy.

You see, Jesus Christ died for you in order to meet your need and comfort your pain. And He is just as alive today and as real as when He walked the shores of Galilee. Make the choice to let Him tenderly love you. All you need to do is ask Him.

His love is just the whisper of a prayer away. Why not bow your head and pray this prayer right now?

A BIBLE CURE PRAYER
FOR YOU

Dear Jesus, thank You for the great love You have for me. Thank You that You died for me to give me salvation, freedom and comfort from all of the anxiety, hurt, emotional pain and turmoil I have experienced throughout my life. I cast my burden before You, and I ask You to reveal Your great love for me in a way that will heal me and comfort me completely. Amen.

Feeling Guilty About Food Cravings?

Have you ever felt that your cravings for certain foods were somehow a guilty reflection upon you? Unhealthy food cravings are merely your body's way of signaling you that something is out of whack. From now on, commit your cravings to God at the moment they occur. He will give you the strength to get through them without

overeating and the grace and wisdom to understand what your body or heart is trying to tell you.
Let your cravings begin a process of bringing your
body back into physical and spiritual balance,
and with that balance, better health.

One of the main emotional motivators that can
send you racing to the refrigerator for comfort is
stress. Stress works against you in other ways, too.

Stress Can Make You Fat

You can improve your lifestyle greatly by reducing
the impact of stress on your body. The excessive
stress that you are under on a daily basis can con-
tribute to obesity. Let me explain. You see, when you
are under stress, your body produces a hormone
called cortisol, which is very similar to cortisone. If
you've ever taken cortisone, you are well aware of
the side effects. Cortisone causes you to gain weight.

Well, cortisol can have the same effect. When
your adrenal glands produce cortisol during
periods of high anxiety and stress, it can actually
cause your body to gain weight. Therefore,
dealing with stress can be a major key in
breaking the bondage of obesity in your life.

Reducing your level of stress can help you lose
weight and keep it off.

77

A Closer Look

Stress affects the heart, the blood vessels and the immune system, but it also directly affects our adrenal glands. The adrenal glands, along with the thyroid gland, help to maintain the body's energy levels.

God's plan for your life will help you to lower your stress. His plan for you is good and not bad. "'For I know the plans I have for you,' says the LORD. 'They are plans for good and not

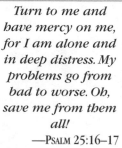

Turn to me and have mercy on me, for I am alone and in deep distress. My problems go from bad to worse. Oh, save me from them all!
—PSALM 25:16–17

for disaster, to give you a future and a hope. In those days when you pray, I will listen. If you look for me in earnest, you will find me when you seek me'" (Jer. 29:11–13).

The Power of Scripture

God's plan for you is for you to surrender your cares to Him and allow His peace to rule in your heart. Begin to memorize and meditate on these two promises for your life:

Don't worry about anything; instead,

pray about everything. Tell God what you
need, and thank him for all he has done.
If you do this, you will experience God's
peace, which is far more wonderful than
the human mind can understand. His
peace will guard your hearts and minds
as you live in Christ Jesus.

—PHILIPPIANS 4:6–7

Give all your worries and cares to God,
for he cares about what happens to you.

—1 PETER 5:7

When you hold on to your worries and cares,
you find yourself under stress and overeating or
not watching what you eat. When you are
depressed and believing that the worst is yet to
come, you may find yourself trying to use food as
comfort. Trust God's Word and plan for your life,
and turn all your cares and worries over to Him.

The Comforter Is Come

In many places in the Bible, the Holy Spirit is
called the Comforter. God knows how tough our
lives can be and how often we must face life's dif-
ficulties alone. That's why He provided Himself as
our Comforter. When the light goes on inside of

your heart, when you really understand that God is real, that He is alive, that you are not alone and that He is able to provide you the comfort you need, you will never reach for the empty comfort of food again.

I encourage you to study the scriptures throughout this booklet; read them over and over again. At the moment you are tempted to reach for comfort from food, read a verse and pray. God is able to give you the strength and help you need to overcome any and all emotional aspects of obesity. He will set you completely free.

The Bread of Life

Jesus says that He is the bread of life. When you feel emotional cravings for sweets, carbohydrates and other foods that you do not need, turn to the bread that you need—Jesus Christ. Let your cravings for rich food be transformed into signals that turn you to true riches in Christ.

Remember His words:

> I am the bread of life. No one who comes to me will ever be hungry again. Those who believe in me will never thirst.
>
> —JOHN 6:35

Conclusion

Remember that you are not dependent on food; you are only dependent upon God. He will give you the strength that you need to overcome sugar addiction. He will also help you understand that food is not your source of comfort or strength—He is!

God is at your side to help you. He promises, "I will never fail you. I will never forsake you" (Heb. 13:5). God is your helper, and food is not your enemy. Your enemies are thoughts, habits and attitudes that tempt you to eat the wrong foods for the wrong reasons. But God gives you a new mind and new attitudes. Already you have started doing things that will effectively help you lose weight. Don't stop now. Pray this Bible Cure prayer and never give up!

A BIBLE CURE PRAYER
FOR YOU

Lord God, You alone are my strength and my source. My ability to stay committed to weight loss and healthy eating comes from You. Help me maintain the will power I need. Give me the focus I need to implement all that I am learning. Almighty God, replace any discouragement with hope and any doubt with faith. I know that You are with me and will not leave me. I thank You, Lord, for seeing me through this battle and giving me victory over obesity. Amen.

A BIBLE CURE PRESCRIPTION

This is a daily checklist to copy and keep on your refrigerator or in your purse or briefcase. Do each one daily for best results.

- ❑ I woke up and prayed, asking for God's help before I got out of bed.
- ❑ I read a scripture verse for God's strength and committed it to memory.
- ❑ I prayed throughout the day, seeking God's continual help and guidance.
- ❑ I ate a balanced breakfast, lunch, dinner and snack according to the Bible Cure plan.
- ❑ I determined to walk in faith today with God's help.
- ❑ I took vitamins and supplements according to the Bible Cure plan.
- ❑ I exercised according to the Bible Cure plan.
- ❑ I feel strong and disciplined with God's help.
- ❑ I thank God throughout the day for victory over obesity.

Conclusion

The Power of God Is Yours

As you've read through this booklet, I hope you've discovered that although God is very powerful, He came to share His power with you. You are not powerless in the face of temptation, fear, loneliness or confusion. One of the most wonderful things about Jesus Christ is that He is very near. He is as close as the whisper of a prayer. Reach out to Him for all of your needs. You will not be disappointed!

—Don Colbert, M.D.

Notes

PREFACE
YOU ARE GOD'S MASTERPIECE!

1. J. F. Balch et al., *Prescription for Nutritional Healing* (Garden Park, NY: Avery Publishing Group, 1997).
2. H. L. Steward et al., *Sugar Busters* (New York: Ballantine Books, 1998), 246.
3. Saundra Macd. Hunter, Ph.D., Julie A. Larrieu, Ph.D., F. Merritt Ayad, Ph.D., et al., "Roles of Mental Health Professionals in Multidisciplinary Medically Supervised Treatment Programs for Obesity," *Southern Medical Journal* (June, 1997), http://www.sma.org/smj/97 june2.htm.
4. Ibid.

CHAPTER 1
DID YOU KNOW?—UNDERSTANDING OBESITY

1 Steward, *Sugar Busters*.

Don Colbert, M.D., was born in Tupelo, Mississippi. He attended Oral Roberts School of Medicine in Tulsa, Oklahoma, where he received a bachelor of science degree in biology in addition to his degree in medicine. Dr. Colbert completed his internship and residency with Florida Hospital in Orlando, Florida. He is board certified in family practice and has received extensive training in nutritional medicine.

If you would like more
information about natural and
divine healing, or information about
Divine Health Nutritional Products ®,
you may contact
Dr. Colbert at:

DR. DON COLBERT

1908 Boothe Circle
Longwood, FL 32750
Telephone: 407-331-7007

Dr. Colbert's Web site is
www.drcolbert.com.